STEVE PARISH

Sydney
AUSTRALIA

STEVE PARISH PUBLISHING PTY LTD

Introduction

Beautiful, vivacious Sydney glitters with a seductive charm which captivates the visitor. Set around Port Jackson, one of the world's finest harbours and natural waterways, this multicultural metropolis is a dynamic business capital, a major international travel destination and a great place to live. Sydney is home to nearly one-quarter of Australia's population, its suburbs expanding across the plains westward to the mountains, and stretching north and south over hilly terrain to meld with the adjacent cities of Gosford and Wollongong.

The cluster of office towers in the central business district give the city a compact, accessible atmosphere in a dramatically beautiful geographical setting. Those fortunate commuters travelling to the city by ferry early on a sparkling morning cross shimmering water beneath a deep blue, bright sky. The brilliance of this light is Sydney's trademark.

Until recent years the old buildings not so much mixed with the new as held their ground until further development encroached. Fortunately, many architectural gems remain and fit well with their new neighbours. The famed Sydney Opera House, for instance, was designed to complement its spectacular harbourside location and, like the Harbour Bridge, has become a Sydney icon. On a more human scale, at The Rocks, where European settlement began in Australia, many old buildings have been preserved and cobbled streets restored. As a botanical delight, the harbourside Royal Botanic Gardens abut the city and offer a haven from the commercial hurly-burly of day-to-day life in the central business district.

The city has a vigorous, somewhat hybrid, cultural and intellectual life that fosters the avant garde and the traditional in music, theatre and art. While the Opera House offers live theatre, opera, ballet, dance and classical music, there are many other venues which cater for everything from established theatre to fringe performance art. The Art Gallery of New South Wales, the major state showcase for Australian and international art, augments its permanent exhibitions with blockbuster shows. As well, the Museum of Contemporary Art, Australia's first major museum for the international arts, enriches the city's art scene.

An integral part of the ethos of Sydney is an affinity with its waterways and with the ocean. I spent eight years in the navy based at Rushcutters Bay and I never ceased to marvel at the number of sailing boats on the harbour at any time of the year and the large crowds on the harbour and ocean beaches. A mixture of subtropical and temperate climates means relatively mild summers and winters and ensures that everything from surfing to bushwalking to picnicking is possible year-round.

Even the less energetic will be pottering around in their beloved back yards, perhaps gardening or planning a barbecue. Sydneysiders are as passionate as any Australians about sport, and just about every competitive sport ever invented is played somewhere in Sydney, from lawn bowls to lawn tennis.

Naturally, not everyone heads for the great outdoors. Sydney has urban precincts, particularly in the inner city, each with its own distinct cultural style. The city's stylish cafe society can be found at the many tables which spill onto footpaths. Darlinghurst, Paddington, Bondi, Glebe, Newtown and Leichhardt are renowned for night clubs, pubs, cafes and upmarket specialty shops. Kings Cross, originally a bohemian haunt, now famous for its glittering night-life, is one of the most densely populated places in Australia. Eating out in the city or any of the inner city suburbs is a culinary treat as diners select from a wide range of international cuisines. Many restaurants are equal to the world's best.

For shoppers, Sydney's central business district is the retail mecca. Refurbished old complexes such as the Queen Victoria Building have been transformed into prestigious shopping venues. Some streets have been blocked to traffic so that pedestrians can safely roam the numerous shopping arcades, many linked with the department stores. Sydney Tower, which rises above Centrepoint, is the ideal spot for a bird's-eye view of the beauty of the city and surrounds: the ocean, suburbia and the far-away mountains. Darling Harbour, a convention and shopping centre on the waterfront just to the west of the city centre, surrounded by landscaped gardens and walkways, teems with tourists and sightseeing suburbanites any fine weekend.

Sydney is surrounded by a variety of ecological wonders including coastlands, rainforests, mountain ranges and river valleys, all protected by one of the largest near-city national park systems in the world. These refuges for native plants and animals also provide respite for day-trippers and are the lungs of the urban environment. To the west of the city is the visual splendour of the sublime sandstone cliffs and forested grand canyons of the Blue Mountains; while to the south, Royal National Park features glorious coastal scenery, discrete rainforests and natural river systems. Northwards, the waterways around Broken Bay rival those of Port Jackson for size and magnificence.

Friendly, cosmopolitan and livable, Sydney has few peers. As host city for the 2000 Olympics, it is gearing up to be the showcase for the nation. While exploring its multi-talented populace, it retains a laid-back, yet vital, style which is uniquely Australian and inspires visitors to return for more of what the city has on offer. It is truly one of the world's great cities.

Steve Parish

Contents

The Sydney Skyline

In recent times Sydney experienced an office building boom which has altered the skyline from year to year. As well, residential complexes are breathing new life into the central business district, bringing the city alive outside office hours. The compact nature of the CBD, bordered by Circular Quay, Darling Harbour and the Royal Botanic Gardens, makes Sydney a most accessible city.

Above: The city skyline and freeway viewed from the Cahill Expressway.
Opposite Above: The Harbour Bridge and city skyline at night.
Opposite Below: Night time city skyline from Potts Point.
Pages 20-21: Night time city view from the old Pyrmont Bridge.
Pages 22-23: A view over Farm Cove, the Royal Botanic Gardens, Government House and the city.

The Sydney Tower

Sydney Tower, the tallest structure in the city, rises above Centrepoint Shopping Centre. The observation deck is an ideal place to get a 360 degree view of the city and suburbs; on a clear day it is possible to see as far as the Blue Mountains in the west. Diners in the three revolving restaurants are slowly and gently treated to the full panorama. The Monorail runs in a one-way, anti-clockwise loop from Darling Harbour, past the Sydney Convention Centre, Haymarket, Chinatown and Pitt Street back towards Darling Harbour. It may not cover the entire city but passengers can explore the western edge and retail districts travelling in style and comfort above the traffic.

Above: The Sydney Tower and surrounding buildings silhouetted by the glow of dusk.
Opposite: With the Sydney Tower in the background, the Monorail turns into Market Street towards Darling Harbour.
Pages 24-25: The Oriana escorted up the harbour to its berth at Circular Quay.

The Queen Victoria Building

Built in 1898 as a produce market, the Queen Victoria Building languished as government offices before restoration in 1986 to one of the finest shopping centres in the world. More than 200 specialty shops occupy the five levels. The building has a variety of artefacts associated with Queen Victoria. The impressive clock, the centre-piece of the building's interior, chimes on the hour. Above the clockface is a revolving historical tableau depicting the lives of Kings and Queens of England dating back to the 11th century.

Top: At night the Victorian splendour of the Queen Victoria Building contrasts with the starkness of the office towers.
Bottom: The magnificent reproduction stained-glass windows facing George Street are based on the original designs.
Opposite: Looking down from the top level of the Queen Victoria Building.

The impressive Sydney Town Hall, completed in 1889, illuminated at night.

A view down George Street towards Central Railway with the cinema complexes and Planet Hollywood.

The splendid interior of St Mary's Cathedral. Designed in the Gothic revival style
and started last century, St Mary's is the spiritual home of Sydney's Roman Catholics.
Located just across the road from Hyde Park, the church is still awaiting the spires that were part of the original design.

The portico of the Art Gallery of New South Wales. Showcasing the best of Australian art,
the Gallery also has a broad selection of international art from Europe, the United States and Asia.
The recently opened Gallery of Aboriginal Art houses some excellent examples of traditional and contemporary indigenous art.

Top left and right: The old reflects the new: Centrepoint Tower and its reflection in a window.
Bottom left and right; Opposite: The Rocks and the city reflected.

Walking around Sydney

The central business district of Sydney is compact and is easily explored on foot. The observant pedestrian will enjoy the variety of public art encountered along the way. From the centre of the the city it is only a short walk to Darling Harbour, Chinatown, The Rocks, the Opera House and the Royal Botanic Gardens. There are several pedestrian malls including the Pitt Street Mall and Martin Plaza. From Circular Quay a harbour walkway links The Rocks with the Royal Botanic Gardens.

Top left: Mural, Oxford Street, Paddington. *Top right:* Walkway, Darling Harbour.
Bottom: A footbridge to Darling Harbour.
Opposite: Looking up at Governor Phillip Tower from the forecourt of the Museum of Sydney with the sculpture 'The Edge of the Trees' by Fiona Foley and Janet Lawrence.

Shopping in Sydney

For serious shoppers, Sydney's central business district is the place to go. Pedestrians roam the numerous shopping arcades lining Pitt Street Mall which are linked with large department stores. Nearby, Queen Victoria Building has been transformed into a prestigious shopping venue to match the classic Victorian-era Strand Arcade between Pitt and George Streets. Retail centres such as Centrepoint, Skygarden and the Glasshouse can also be found in Pitt Street Mall along with hundreds of specialty shops. Further downtown, The Rocks, with many restored cobbled laneways, caters for tourists. In recent years many exclusive brand-name shops have opened branches in the city. Darling Harbour, a convention, exhibition and shopping centre on the waterfront, just to the west of the city centre, is surrounded by landscaped gardens and walkways. In the inner suburbs there are excellent shopping precincts with specialty stores in Double Bay, Paddington, Woollahra, Glebe, Newtown and Chatswood.

Above: The Pitt Street Mall, in the centre of the city, is a popular lunchtime spot for office workers.
Opposite: The historic Strand Arcade, with its high Victorian iron balustrading and arched glass roof, runs between Pitt Street Mall and George Street.

Top left: Creperie Stivell, Five Ways, Paddington. *Top right:* The Tea Centre of Sydney, Glenmore Road, Paddington.
Bottom left: The Country Trader, Glenmore Road, Paddington. *Bottom right:* Queen Street Fruit Market, Woollahra.

Above: DeCosti Seafoods, Sydney Fish Markets, Pyrmont.
Below: Orson and Blake Collectables, Queen Street, Woollahra.

Chinatown

Chinatown, centred on Dixon Street at the southern end of the city, is only a short walk from Darling Harbour. This unique part of Sydney comes to life in the evenings with the colourful display of lights and the bustle of evening crowds exploring the myriad of shops and restaurants. Prominent among the visitors are those food aficionados who come to seek out the specialist regional Chinese cuisines. The city's fruit and vegetable market was located nearby until recent years, although part of the old market is now the site of the popular Paddy's Market - the place to go for bargains from the hundreds of stallholders who set up here on trading days.

Above: A smiling staff member welcomes customers to one of the many Chinese restaurants in Dixon Street.
Opposite: The Chinatown mall, shown at one of the very rare times when it is not thronged with pedestrians.

The Royal Botanic Gardens

The harbourside Royal Botanic Gardens, on the site of the original Government Farm and adjoining the east of the city centre, is the city's gem. Over 30 hectares of magnificent gardens include wide expanses of lawn with colourful beds of exotic and native plants, and two glasshouses containing tropical ferns, orchids and palms. The walk beginning from Mrs Macquaries Chair, on the eastern point of Farm Cove, around the Cove to the Opera House, would be the finest of all of Sydney's walking tours. Nearby, historic Macquarie Street has some of Sydney's few remaining buildings of colonial heritage, the State Parliament House, and the more recent imposing State Library.

Above: The Captain Arthur Phillip statue and fountain, Royal Botanic Gardens.
Opposite: The Royal Botanic Gardens, looking towards the city with the new Chifley Square Tower on the right.

The art-deco Anzac War Memorial dominates the southern section of Hyde Park.

The statue of Apollo atop the Archibald Fountain, the centrepiece of the northern section of Hyde Park.

The Sydney Opera House

Located on Bennelong Point, to the east of Circular Quay, the Sydney Opera house is regarded by many as one of the world's greatest public buildings. It was designed in 1956 by the Danish architect, Jorn Utzon, to complement its spectacular harbourside location. The building was not completed until 1973 after a series of disputes which saw Utzon resign and the project brought to completion by a team of local architects. The Opera House is actually the venue for live theatre, opera, ballet, modern dance and classical music, although its sightseeing tours are as popular as any of its performances. The smaller 'shell', on the left at the top of the imposing front stairway, is an exclusive restaurant.

Above: The Sydney Opera House from west Circular Quay with a ferry in the foreground.
Opposite: A pianist rehearsing in the Concert Hall, Sydney Opera House.
Pages 50-51: At dusk, the lights appear to tip the sails of the Opera House with gold.

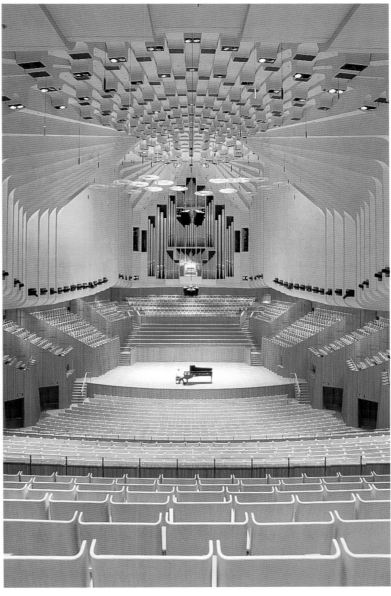

A misty-morning view of the Opera House and the Harbour Bridge from Mrs Macquaries Chair.

An evening view of the Opera House and the Harbour Bridge from Mrs Macquaries Chair.

Above: Sydney's twin icons, the Opera House and Harbour Bridge, viewed from Mrs Macquaries Chair.
Opposite: Mrs Macquaries Chair, on the eastern point of Farm Cove, is a favoured vantage point
to observe and photograph the Opera House and the Harbour Bridge.
Pages 54-55: The city is often enlivened when a cruise ship is in port. Here the Oriana berths at the Overseas Passenger Terminal.
Pages 58-59: The Opera House appears to float on the harbour when viewed from west Circular Quay in the evening.

The Rocks

A short walk from Circular Quay, The Rocks is the site of the first European settlement in Australia. Convicts from the First Fleet in 1788 cleared the area which gained the name 'The Rocks' because of its sandstone outcrops. Today, thanks to the efforts of conservationists who rejected a plan which would have seen the area levelled for high-rise development, many of the buildings have been restored. Pubs and restaurants mingle with art and craft galleries, boutiques, specialty and gift shops which showcase Australian products such as opals, glassware, sheepskin products and Aboriginal art.

Top: 'Sydney's Oldest Hotel', the Lord Nelson in the Rocks, has been serving patrons since early last century.
Bottom: Cadman's Cottage, Sydney's oldest house, is located in George Street.
Opposite top: The low-rise buildings at The Rocks are a welcome contrast to the city towers.
Opposite bottom: A Playfair Street sculpture celebrating pioneer life.

Top left: Dorian Scott, George Street. *Top right:* Pizzeria, George Street.
Bottom left: Cafe, Playfair Street. *Bottom right:* Building detail, The Rocks.
Opposite: The Palisade Hotel, The Rocks.

These restored bond houses at The Rocks have been converted into restaurants.

Restored bond warehouses, The Rocks, looking north towards the Harbour Bridge.

Circular Quay

Circular Quay, the main terminus within the city for ferries, buses and trains, is the embarkation point for harbour cruises. The sights of Port Jackson can also be enjoyed from Sydney's commuter ferries which provide relaxed and unhurried transportation to harbour suburbs such as Manly, Watsons Bay, Mosman, Balmain and Parramatta. A harbourside walkway links The Rocks, the Opera House, the Museum of Modern Art and the Royal Botanic Gardens.

Above: Sculptures, Circular Quay.
Opposite: Circular Quay walkway, looking north towards the Overseas Passenger Terminal and the Harbour Bridge.
Pages 68-69: An aerial view of the city, looking south over Circular Quay, the busy ferry terminus. The Oriana is berthed at the Overseas Passenger Terminal. On the left are the Conservatorium of Music and the Royal Botanic Gardens.

The HMAV Bounty

Built for the movie 'The Bounty', starring Mel Gibson, Sydney's HMAV Bounty is an exact-size, fully-rigged replica of Bligh's original vessel. The three masts are made from British Columbian Pine with the main one 40 metres tall. The vessel is 42 metres long and weighs 400 tonnes. Apart from film work, the ship participated in the First Fleet re-enactment in 1988, and the following year was sailed to the South Pacific to re-enact the 200-year anniversary of the original mutiny. Today, the ship is berthed at historic Campbells Cove at The Rocks. Her concessions to modernity are all below deck and include twin turbo-charged marine diesel engines. HMAV Bounty sails Sydney Harbour every day of the year, giving locals and visitors alike a taste of eighteenth-century adventure with twentieth-century dining.

Above: HMAV Bounty carrying sightseers on Sydney Harbour.
Opposite: HMAV Bounty moored at Campbells Cove with the Opera House in the background.

The Sydney Harbour Bridge

Known affectionately by locals as 'The Coat-hanger', the Sydney Harbour Bridge was considered an engineering feat when it was completed in 1932. Spanning the harbour between Dawes Point at The Rocks and Milsons Point at North Sydney, the highest part of the arch rises 134 metres above the water, the deck is 49 metres wide and the massive steel structure carries 15 000 vehicles per hour during peak hour. The south-eastern pylon is open for sightseers, and the bridge itself is accessible from The Rocks to pedestrians who wish to walk across the harbour.

Above: Looking towards the Harbour Bridge from east Circular Quay on a calm summer's evening.
Opposite: A passenger vessel berthed at the Overseas Passenger Terminal, with the city lights as a backdrop.

Darling Harbour

Darling Harbour, just to the west of the city centre, is the place to go for shopping and dining. Once railway goods yards, the redevelopment has put new heart into the city as a weekend destination for thousands of people who flock to the exhibition, convention and shopping complexes surrounded by landscaped gardens and walkways. Nearby, the Sydney Aquarium, National Maritime Museum and Powerhouse Museum are major attractions. The old Pyrmont Bridge, now a pedestrian walkway, links the city.

Top: Flags silhouetted in the morning sun.
Bottom: Looking towards the red and blue glass of Segaworld, an indoor family amusement park at Darling Harbour, replete with rides, live entertainment and arcade games.
Opposite: The northern edge of Darling Harbour looking east along the old Pyrmont Bridge to the city and Sydney Tower. The monorail runs across here on its city circuit.

Cockle Bay Wharf

Cockle Bay Wharf is a welcome addition to Darling Harbour's many attractions. This large complex, on the city side of Darling Harbour, is famous for its fabulous variety of restaurants and cafés. Dining experiences can be as simple or as extravagant as the visitor desires, and al fresco dining on a warm evening is a pleasure not to be missed. The waters of Cockle Bay play host to spectacular film and laser shows enthralling audiences with holographic-like images, and the nearby Panasonic IMAX Theatre has "the world's biggest movie screen".

Above: City buildings form the backdrop to the eastern side of Darling Harbour, where Cockle Bay Wharf is located.
Opposite: Cockle Bay Wharf complements the original Darling Harbour development. The structure in the distance with the yellow and black checkerboard design is the Panasonic IMAX Theatre.

Top: The Sydney Aquarium, Darling Harbour. One of the world's largest aquariums,
it features a diverse collection of Australian aquatic life, including reef fish,
saltwater crocodiles and a large collection of sharks. Visitors walk through 146
metres of underwater glass tunnels, as the marine life swims around them.
Bottom: Looking over the Sydney Aquarium along the western
edge of the central business district.

Top: A pagoda on a corner of the Chinese Gardens, Darling Harbour.
Bottom: The entrance to the Chinese Gardens.
Pages 76-77: The old Manly ferry the 'South Steyne', moored on the eastern edge of
Darling Harbour, is an information centre for the 2000 Olympics, to be held in Sydney.

The National Maritime Museum

The National Maritime Museum, at Darling Harbour, has been established to show how closely Australians are linked to the sea. Its exhibitions explore some of the major influences on Australian life including Aboriginal culture, successive waves of immigration, the development of coastal commerce and industry, defence at sea, aquatic sports and seaside recreation. A special gallery recalls two centuries of maritime contact between the USA and Australia. Moored at its wharves, the Museum's 12 historic vessels range from a Vietnamese refugee boat to a naval destroyer.

Above: An aerial view of the Maritime Museum looking west over Pyrmont and Blackwattle Bay towards the western suburbs.
Opposite top: A display of maritime signal flags in front of the National Maritime Museum with the monorail crossing Pyrmont Bridge.
Opposite bottom: The entrance of the National Maritime Museum.

The Harbour Lights

Sydneysiders love a fireworks show; the best displays bejewel the skies over Sydney Harbour, whose waters dance with the sparkle of reflected colours. Spectacular annual fireworks celebrate New Year's Eve, although any occasion is an excuse for a celebration. The illuminated office buildings and city lights also provide a fine spectacle when reflected in the harbour. There are good vantage points for views of the city from Darling Harbour and Circular Quay. As well, a night trip on a ferry offers the chance to see not only city lights, but also the illuminated residences along the harbour foreshores.

Above left: Fireworks display, Sydney Harbour. *Above right:* A view from the pedestrian access bridge, Darling Harbour, with the city behind.
Opposite top: Star City, a harbourside complex combining an assortment of attractions, including gaming, theatres, and a five-star hotel.
Opposite bottom: Looking west towards Darling Harbour from the city.

Looking West

The new Glebe Island Bridge is the gateway to Sydney's northwestern suburbs. The roadway is suspended by lines of cables anchored to the tops of two massive concrete towers. The old opening bridge is dwarfed by the new structure which offers fine views over the inner western suburbs and Blackwattle Bay. Sydney's west is the growth region and new suburbs feed an urban sprawl stretching towards the Blue Mountains. Parramatta and Penrith have developed into important retail and commercial centres, while in the southwest, Liverpool and Campbelltown are cities in their own right.

Above: The new Glebe Island Bridge from Rozelle Bay at dusk.
Opposite: Travelling towards the city on the new Glebe Island Bridge.

Above left: An aerial view over Drummoyne and the Gladesville Bridge, looking west down the Parramatta River.
Above right: Looking over Long Nose Point, Birchgrove, to the west along the Parramatta River.
Opposite: Five Dock Point with the Parramatta River in the foreground, Five Dock Bay
behind and the suburbs of Chiswick, Abbotsford and Five Dock in the background.

Olympic Park

At Homebush Bay, 16 kilometres west of the city centre, the Olympic sports facilities are designed to be state-of-the-art. The most spectacular of these is Stadium Australia, which, with a crowd capacity of 110 000, is the largest of any outdoor Olympic stadium. Adjacent to the Homebush Bay site an Olympic Village has been specially designed to house the athletes. Accessible by ferries via the Parramatta River, as well as by road and rail, the central location of the Olympic site means that it is also the perfect venue for the concerts and many sports events enthusiastically supported by Sydneysiders.

Above: Stadium Australia dominates the Homebush Bay Olympic site.
Opposite: An aerial view of Stadium Australia, venue for the opening and closing ceremonies of the XXVII Olympiad.

The Blue Mountains

Two hour's drive west of Sydney, and part of the Great Dividing Range that runs inland along the east coast of Australia, the spectacular scenery of the Blue Mountains is an international tourist destination. The series of towns perched on mountain cliffs, including Leura, Springwood, Katoomba and Blackheath, offer a variety of accommodation, tea rooms, cafes and restaurants, arts and crafts centres and galleries, as well as historic sites. Echo Point at Katoomba is a spectacular place to admire the grandeur and beauty of the mountains. The Blue Mountains National Park is ideal for bushwalking and the mountain towns are starting points for many walks, ranging from half an hour to a full day, to suit all ages and abilities.

Above left: An aerial view over Katoomba, looking over the Jamison Valley.
Above right: Katoomba Scenic Railway, a caged inclinator on rails, descends to the valley below.
Opposite: The Katoomba Scenic Skyway provides superb views of the Three Sisters and the Jamison Valley.

Top: Beauchamp Falls, one of the many spectacular waterfalls in the Blue Mountains.
Bottom: Koalas are found in many parts of Sydney and are often seen on bushland walks.
Opposite: The cooler climate in the Blue Mounatins provides ideal conditions for the planting of carefully designed and tended formal gardens, such as this one in Mt Wilson.

Looking South

Sydney's southern suburbs, which are predominantly residential, stretch all the way to Royal National Park. Many of the houses lining the bays and waterways of the Georges River and Port Hacking have access to the waterways for boating and other water sports. Cronulla, on the coast, has a popular beach, while Bundeena, on the southern side of Port Hacking, is a small town with the charm of a coastal village.

Above: Miranda Fair Shopping Complex, one of Sydney's largest, looking south towards the Hacking River.
Opposite: Aerial view south over the suburbs of Miranda and Yowie Bay, the Hacking River and Royal National Park.
Pages 96-97: An aerial view looking southwest over Cronulla beach, towards the Hacking River and Royal National Park.

South to Wollongong

The industrial city of Wollongong is renowned as the site of the BHP Port Kembla Steelworks and for its extensive nearby coal mines. It sits on the plain between the striking Illawarra Escarpment and the Pacific Ocean. The city was first settled by Europeans early in the nineteenth century when it was known as 'The Garden of New South Wales' for the high quality produce which was grown on the fertile soils. Once large stands of rainforest grew here and there are still remnants in the hidden valleys of the escarpment. Today, Wollongong is a diverse and prosperous city with a university, a regional gallery and a fine botanic garden.

Above: The city of Wollongong with the Illawarra Escarpment.
Opposite: The spectacular coastline looking south to Royal National Park and Wollongong with Semi Detached Point in the foreground.

Looking East

Sydney's eastern suburbs are predominantly prestige residential areas. They are the suburbs in which are found the city's top-priced residences, particularly those with harbour views at Darling Point, Point Piper and Vaucluse. The easy access to such a large expanse of water has meant that sailing clubs are popular while marinas full of every imaginable type of vessel crowd the bays. For shoppers, Double Bay is home to exclusive retail outlets while Rose Bay has a village-like atmosphere. Oxford Street, running from Hyde Park through Darlinghurst and Paddington to Centennial Park, is renowned for its night clubs, pubs, cafes and upmarket specialty shops. The city end of the street bustles with a night life which rivals that of Kings Cross. On the coast, Bondi Beach is a major destination for Sydneysiders looking for somewhere to cool off on a hot summer's day.

Above: Garden Island Dockyards, Potts Point.
Opposite: An aerial view over Sydney's eastern suburbs including Woolloomooloo, Potts Point, Rushcutters Bay, Darling Point, Edgecliff, Double Bay, Rose Bay, Vaucluse and Watsons Bay.

An aerial view looking southeast over Paddington, Surry Hills, Centennial Park, Randwick and, on the coast, Bondi, Coogee and Maroubra. In the centre are the Sydney Cricket Ground and the Sydney Sports Stadium.

Top: Paddington streets are lined with restored terrace houses.
Bottom: The well-known Paddington Bazaar is held on Saturdays. Hundreds of stallholders
sell clothing, arts and crafts and food along with almost anything else you could name.

Kings Cross

Once the haunt of bohemians, Kings Cross is today a diverse pocket of the suburb of Potts Point that really comes to life when the sunlight is displaced by electric and neon lights. 'The Cross', as it is called, is the most densely-populated part of Sydney. The main streets are home to strip clubs and associated retail establishments while many side streets are lined with trees and beautiful old terrace houses. Hotels, boarding houses and backpacker hostels offer accommodation for the many visitors who take advantage of the area's attractions, variety of eating places and its proximity to the city.

Top: Night lights, Darlinghurst Road, Kings Cross.
Bottom: A new version of the famous Harry's Cafe de Wheels, Woolloomooloo.
Opposite: The El Alamein Fountain, long a popular meeting place in Kings Cross.

The Harbour Bays

Some of Sydney's most exclusive residential development is located on the waterfront bordering Port Jackson. In many cases, houses are built clinging to steep hillsides where a precious glimpse of water is regarded as a most desirable attribute. In the dozens of sheltered bays and inlets are moored a myriad of craft which bob around in the wash of passing harbour traffic during the week, being claimed by their owners for weekend sailing or harbour cruising. Here and there are bushland reserves and favoured places for picnics. Sydney Harbour National Park allows public access to much of the harbour foreshore where there are a number of sandy beaches that are popular in summer.

Looking southeast over Vaucluse, Parsley Bay, Vaucluse Bay,
Nielsen Park, Rose Bay with Bondi and the southern beach suburbs in the distance.

Above left: A view of Point Piper looking west towards the city.
Above right: Rose Bay and Dover Heights from the Harbour to the Pacific Ocean.

Aerial view looking southeast over the beach at Camp Cove, Watsons Bay and Vaucluse.

The popular Doyles Restaurant on the beach at Watsons Bay.

Bondi

Bondi Beach, an Australian icon of surf and beach culture, is the most popular suburban beach in Australia. On a summer's day the beach is packed with locals and visitors alike who come to sun themselves and plunge into the cool waters of the Tasman Sea. Shops and cafes line the boulevard that curves around the sandy crescent of the beach. A popular destination with backpackers from all over the world, Bondi and nearby Bondi Junction are cosmopolitan, densely populated residential suburbs with a strong European influence derived from post-war migration.

Above left: An aerial view of Bondi Junction looking southeast towards Waverley and Coogee.
Above right: Looking west over Dover Heights, Bondi Beach towards the city.
Opposite: Bondi Beach is popular with locals and visitors alike on a fine summer's day.
Pages 110-111: An aerial view looking west towards the city over the rocky cliff-face known as The Gap, Watsons Bay and the eastern suburbs.

Surf Lifesaving Carnivals

Bondi's Surf Lifesaving Club was founded in 1906 and is one of the oldest in Australia. In addition to carrying out surf rescues, today's volunteer lifesavers stage immensely popular carnivals which showcase the skills of the surfboat crews, display traditional belt and reel lifesaving techniques, and demonstrate more modern methods of retrieving distressed swimmers. In recent times, women have taken their place in the teams and now number about one-third of the surf lifesaving movement. Highlights of the carnivals are the march-past of lifesavers, and the dramatic surfboat races, an exciting event, particularly when the surf is up.

Above: A surf lifesaving team in the traditional march-past on carnival day.
Opposite: An aerial perspective of surfboats competing in a carnival at Bondi Beach.

Sailing

On any day of the year 'yachties' can be found navigating their vessels of all shapes and sizes on the protected waters of Port Jackson. Taking best advantage of the prevailing winds, the zig-zag patterns of tacking boats add an element of colourful chaos to harbour life. Australia's premier yachting event, the Sydney to Hobart Yacht Race, is held annually, starting on Boxing Day. Boats from all around the world gather in Sydney for the dash down Australia's southeast coast. The fastest boats take a little over two and a half days to make the 1167 kilometre journey. Winners are awarded in both the handicap and line honours categories but, for many, the thrill is in just participating.

Above: With spinnakers billowing, yachts on Sydney Harbour make their way towards the Heads.
Pages 126-127: The big Sydney to Hobart yachts heel over as they pass the red roofs of Sydney's eastern suburbs, on their way to The Heads, before tracking south towards Hobart.

Looking North

Sydney's northern suburbs encompass the mostly residential suburbs which stretch to Hornsby and beyond. A feature of the North Shore, as it is known, is the profusion of trees and shrubs that proud gardeners and local councils have encouraged. North Sydney, a mini-city in its own right, with office towers and retail centres, caters for the daily throng of workers. Further north, Chatswood is a major commercial and retail centre. Along the northern shore of the harbour, houses are built on often steep bushland to take advantage of water views of the more secluded Middle Harbour. On the coast, a string of residential suburbs begins with Manly in the south and includes Dee Why, Narrabeen, Mona Vale and the northern-most exclusive seaside suburb of Palm Beach.

Above: Looking northwest over North Sydney with
Kirribilli, Careening Cove and Neutral Bay in the foreground.
Opposite: An aerial view of North Sydney, Neutral Bay and the
Warringah Expressway looking south towards the city.

An aerial view looking southeast over Wollstonecraft and Waverton to the city and beyond.

An aerial view of Chatswood looking southwest.

Top: Looking east over Middle Harbour, The Spit and the suburbs of Balgowlah and Manly.
Bottom: Looking southwest over Middle Harbour, Beauty Point and Spit Junction to North Sydney and the city.
Opposite: An aerial view over Cammeray with the impressive 'battlements' of Cammeray Bridge.
Pages 132-133: Looking southeast over Mosman and Cremorne, Bradleys Head, Athol Bay, Little Sirius Cove,
Mosman Bay and Robertsons Point, to Rose Bay and the Pacific Ocean.

Taronga Zoo

Set in bushland overlooking Sydney Harbour, Taronga Zoological Park has one of the most spectacular settings in the world in which to view the animals. In keeping with a modern zoo's code of presenting exhibits in as natural a setting as possible, staff now care for animals which are well presented and comfortable. Taronga also participates in breeding programs that endeavour to prevent the extinction of endangered species.

Top: Looking towards Cremorne Point and the city from the zoo.
Bottom: Taronga's giraffes have one of the best views over the Harbour.
Opposite: The Elephant House, with the city in the background.

Manly

The seaside suburb of Manly with its beaches, its shaded mall, its restaurants and boutiques has always been a popular destination for Sydneysiders. The trip there on the ferry is not a small part of the pleasure of the visit. Manly also attracts visitors for sheer entertainment which includes everything from surf carnivals to street concerts. In fact, it is a great place to sit, soak up the sun and watch the world go by.

Above: The popular Corso which runs down to Manly Beach.
Below: Public art and a pedestrian mall make the Corso a favourite place for visitors.
Opposite: An aerial view looking south over North Steyne and Manly beaches towards the harbour and the eastern suburbs.
Pages 138-139: Looking over the sandstone cliffs of North Head towards the harbour entrance, South Head and the city.

Looking north over Manly, with the wharf in the foreground.

Looking south over Manly towards the eastern suburbs.

The Central Coast

The Central Coast, for many years a popular holiday destination, is fast becoming a dormitory suburb for Sydney. The main city, Gosford, has the advantage of being located on Brisbane Water, a large expanse of water north of Broken Bay, and is accessible by freeway from the northern suburbs of Sydney. Close to excellent surf beaches and national parks, the Central Coast boasts the resorts of Terrigal, The Entrance and Toukley.

Above: Looking south over Gosford towards Brisbane Water.
Opposite: The popular holiday resort, The Entrance, situated north of Gosford at the opening to Tuggerah Lake.

Above left: Avoca Beach. *Above:* Terrigal Beach.
Pages 158-159: A lone fisherman on Frazer Beach, Munmorah State Recreation Park.

Acknowledgements

I n a book such as this it is possible to depict only some of the visual delights the city and environs have to offer. While I chose those images that seem to me to represent the essence of Sydney, I could easily have filled a second book with pictures of this beautiful city.

I am indebted to Phillip Hayson for his assistance with the photography, particularly for his photographs on the dust jacket, pages 6–7, 74 (bottom), 74–5, 76, 77, 82 (top), 83 (right), 88 and 89; the Photo Library of Australia for the photograph by David Messent, page 49; Rod Ritchie for the text and Pip McConnel-Oats for the elegant design.

STEVE PARISH CASEBOUND BOOK COLLECTION

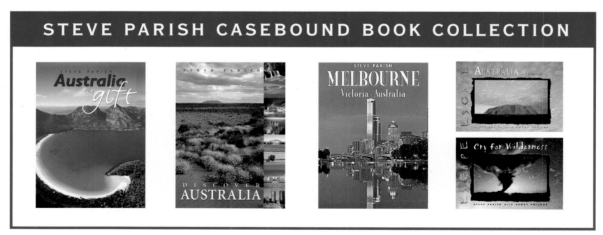

AVAILABLE AT ALL GOOD BOOKSTORES AND STEVE PARISH STOCKISTS

Steve Parish
PUBLISHING

© copyright Steve Parish Publishing Pty Ltd
PO Box 1058, Archerfield, Queensland 4108 Australia
ISBN 1875932 64 X
Printed in China at Everbest Printing Co. Ltd
**Designed, produced and published in Australia
by Steve Parish Publishing Pty Ltd**
www.steveparish.com.au